Your
Spiritual Weapons
and
How to Use Them

by

Terry Law

VICTORY HOUSE, INC.
Tulsa, Oklahoma

Unless otherwise indicated, all Scripture quotations are taken from the *King James Version* of the Bible.

Your Spiritual Weapons and How to Use Them
ISBN 0-932081-00-2
Copyright © 1983 by Terry Law
Terry Law Ministries
P.O. Box 92
Tulsa, Oklahoma 74101

Published by VICTORY HOUSE, INC.
P.O. Box 700238
Tulsa, Oklahoma 74170

Contents

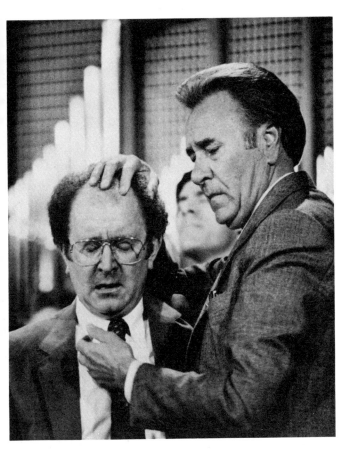

"Terry, God bless my prayer with you and enable you to fulfill your total calling. All my love and affection — Oral."

1
God Is Moving By His Spirit

For though we walk in the flesh, we do not war after the flesh.

(For the weapons of our warfare are not carnal, but mighty through God to the pulling down of strongholds;)

Casting down imaginations, and every high thing that exalteth itself against the knowledge of God, and bringing into captivity every thought to the obedience of Christ.

2 Corinthians 10:3-5

I began what was to become the current wave of my ministry in 1969 on the campus of Oral Roberts University. It was during that year that I received my degree from ORU and formed a musical team called Living Sound. When several others and I came up with the idea for a musical group we did not intend for it to become a full-time ministry; it was just going to be something that we did on weekends. But in our first series of meetings in a charismatic Baptist Church in Kansas City, Missouri, the Lord spoke to us and said, ''I want this ministry to go to Africa.'' So we went to Africa where we spent a full year in ministry.

In Poland

It was while our team was ministering in Africa that a strange thing happened to me. I was praying behind the stage before going out to lead the service one evening. I was kneeling on a rug with my Bible open in front of me. While I was praying in the Spirit, getting ready to go out and minister to the congregation, I had an encounter with God so supernatural that it shook me to the core of my being.

Suddenly, I could sense that the Lord was in the room with me, and for the first time in my life I heard God speak. This was not an inner voice, not a witness in my spirit; I heard the audible voice of God. I didn't hear it with my ears, but my entire body was vibrating with the sound that was around me.

As the Lord spoke to me, He said, ''Son, I'm going to send you behind the Iron Curtain. You're going to do things there that most people will believe impossible, but you must be obedient and follow Me implicitly.''

Now I had been behind the Iron Curtain a year or two earlier, and I didn't like it. I didn't want to go back there, so I argued with the Lord. But it's hard to argue under those circumstances. I had perhaps 30 minutes while the team was finishing their music before I was to preach. During that time I argued, but I was getting nowhere. Finally, it came time for me to go out and speak.

When I put my Bible on the pulpit, opened it, and prepared to read my text, I was in rebellion against the Lord. Every time I tried to read a word out loud, nothing would come out of my mouth. After several minutes of looking the fool, I decided that I had better give in to the Lord. So in front of that audience I made an announcement. I said, "I would like to announce that this ministry, Living Sound, is going behind the Iron Curtain. I don't know when and I don't know how. But we are going."

I didn't tell them that I didn't want to go. I just said that we were going. There were many gasps from the audience, but most of them came from Living Sound members standing behind me.

But I told the Lord that I would not solicit an invitation. I said that I would not make any attempt to get us there on our own. I told Him that if He wanted us to go, it was His plan, and He would have to open the door. And so we waited.

For two years nothing happened, and I was rejoicing in the Lord. We were enjoying our ministry in the United States and in other parts of the world. Then all of a sudden one day, out of the blue, a letter came to us from Poland. It was an official invitation to us to come and sing on a university campus, the Jagiellonian University in Krakow, in the southern part of the nation of Poland.

When I received that letter, I felt the witness of the Spirit within me. I knew that God was saying, "I want you to go minister there." So, we accepted the invitation and made our plans to go. We were on our way to Israel and back to

Africa again that fall, and when we arrived in Poland, I found out much to my dismay that two terrible mistakes had been made.

First of all, we were extended an invitation to come and sing because the organizers of the event had somehow mixed us up with another group. They thought we were an American rock 'n roll group. The second mistake was that they had scheduled us to do a fund-raising benefit in the headquarters of the Communist Party. The young men who had invited us were not university students, they were leaders of the youth Communist movement in southern Poland.

We were scheduled for two concerts in the Party headquarters the next day. I cannot describe the tensions we felt as we walked into that room to perform. The air was blue with smoke, there were beer bottles sitting around every place, and we could sense a distinctly non-Christian atmosphere. So Living Sound got up to sing. Now our repertoire was definitely limited — we only knew how to sing about Jesus. We also knew that sooner or later these people were going to realize what we were singing about. So we held a hasty strategy meeting and came to the decision that after about three songs I would get up and impress the gathering with my vast knowledge of Polish history. Sure enough, after three songs the natives were getting restless, so I got up and began to talk about Poland. I ran out of information in about 30 to 60 seconds. I just stood there wondering what was about to happen. I whispered to the Lord, ''What do I do now?''

The Lord said, ''What do you think I brought you here for?'' And something began to well up inside of me. I opened my mouth and boldly declared to the audience: ''Marx and Lenin do not have the way. There is only one way, and His name is Jesus Christ.'' And then I began to declare the Gospel. I gave them an outline of the plan of salvation and expressed how Christ had changed my life by His power and grace.

When I walked off the stage, two men were waiting for me. They grabbed me under both arms and escorted me off while the group was still singing. I was ushered into the basement where I was interrogated for at least 45 minutes or longer. I won't reveal what was said down there, because it should not be repeated in polite company.

First of all, these agents thought that we were part of the CIA. They accused us of working for the American government. Then they accused me of trying to indoctrinate Communist youth, of spreading subversive propaganda. They threatened my life. All this went on for what seemed an eternity. Finally, I was able to convince them that we weren't political spies, but just a group of singers. They were still obviously upset and suspicious, but they agreed to let me go back and join the group.

''But,'' they warned me sternly, ''No more

talking.'' They said that they had taken in so much money on our performance that they were embarrassed not to let us continue to perform. But under no circumstances were we to be allowed to talk!

I said, ''That's fine.''

So the group and I came back on stage to sing. In fact, the rest of the team had kept right on singing while I was downstairs. They were all praying for me while they sang. They were wondering if we were ever going to see freedom again.

We were scheduled for two concerts that evening, one at 5:00 p.m., the other at 7:00 p.m. During the second concert, something happened. I've never seen anything like it in my life. A lot of our music at that time was contemporary, upbeat, and we were impressing the crowd with the professional quality of our music and performance. Suddenly, I sensed the Holy Spirit do something that totally astonished me.

The music changed. We began to move into praise and worship, and some of our young people began to lift their hands in praise to the Lord. I saw tears start to steal down the cheeks of some of those who were worshipping the Lord. All of a sudden I turned around and looked at the audience, and I saw that they were mesmerized. Nobody was clapping anymore, nobody was keeping time to the music, their eyes were glued on the young people on stage.

They could not believe what they were seeing. They were watching American and Canadian young people, with their hands in the air, worshipping God — and they didn't know what to do or say.

For the next few minutes there was dead silence in the audience as we sang and worshipped openly and freely. The anointing had struck the room with such power that we had a slide trombone player who was playing his instrument with one hand in the air. (Try that sometime if you are a musician!)

The last song we sang was "God Is Moving By His Spirit, Moving Through All the Earth." As the music faded away there was about 15 to 30 seconds of dead silence. I was scared. During that ominous silence I was fervently praying in the Spirit, "Lord, do something!" Then suddenly, in one body, the audience leaped to their feet and began to applaud. They began to respond exuberantly, moving toward the front of the room. We were there until 3:30 in the morning leading people to Christ.

The Lord was giving me a signal in the Spirit, at that point, but I didn't pick up on it as quickly as I should have. After that experience, we waited for a while before returning behind the Iron Curtain. Then we went back to Poland in 1974.

Among the Catholics

The Lord spoke to me in a meeting we were

having in Tampa, Florida, and told me in a supernatural way that we were to minister in the Roman Catholic Church. I had great difficulty accepting that because of some experiences I had had with the Catholic Church earlier in my life. I found it hard to believe that the Lord was actually sending me to minister to Catholics in their own churches.

However, I noticed that when we went back to Poland the doors were opened for us to minister in Catholic churches. It almost seemed miraculous. When we arrived we had no bookings at all. We just got on our bus, drove into the country and said, "Lord, it's up to You," and the Lord opened the door.

We phoned the head priest of St. Anne's Cathedral in downtown Warsaw, Father George, and told him, "We're in town and we'd like to sing."

"Good, good," he said, "Come on and sing for Mass on Thursday night."

Now I had never been to Mass before and I really didn't know what to do, so we just did as the Lord led us. I'm sure those people had a Mass like they'd never had before in their lives. But it was effective.

When I walked out for service, there were about 2,500 people jammed wall to wall in that church. After we had sung and ministered, I gave an invitation for people to accept Christ, and 350 people met me in the sacristy on the side of the sanctuary. Later Cardinal Primate

Wyszynski called us on the phone to say, "If you will come, I will open every cathedral in Poland to you. The communists are running the country, including the school system. They are teaching our children that God is dead. But the young people are listening to you, to your music. If you will only come, we will open every church in our nation to you."

I noticed that in our meetings in the Roman Catholic churches that something special began to happen when we moved into an atmosphere of worship and praise. I would have the audience stand and hold hands together and we would sing the chorus, "Hallelujah." Then we would worship the Lord.

I remember a service we held in the city of Czestochowa, where the shrine of the Black Madonna is located. There were 250,000 people gathered in an outdoor field. Living Sound sang and I preached for about 30 or 40 minutes. We shared the Gospel, and then we had the people hold their hands together and worship the Lord. They began to weep and cry as the anointing of the Holy Spirit fell upon them. Again the Lord was giving me a signal.

In Russia

In 1979 I took a team to Moscow, Russia. As we were on our way to the city we had an accident in the middle of a snowstorm. We were driving down the road in our own bus, when suddenly a truck came looming out of the storm right at us. The truck came so close to our bus that its side mirror smashed the front window of our bus, knocking one of our young men flat on his back down the aisle. We had to stop and get an iron plate put in the window to keep out the cold.

We had been scheduled to arrive about 6:00 p.m., but it was around 11:00 by the time we finally got there. Viktor, our underground contact, was at the hotel when the bus rolled in. He said, "You're not going to believe it, but I've got a concert scheduled for you in place called the Red Star Club." He told us that this club was just about five minutes from Lenin's tomb and that the top musicians of the country were there — including Mockfudava, the lady who had composed the theme song for the Russian Olympics.

"There are ballet dancers, artists, poets, musicians, writers there," he said. "They've been waiting since 7:00 p.m. It's 11:00 now, but they are insisting on a concert. It doesn't matter when you start, just get there!"

By the time the team got set up to perform it was 1:00 a.m. We sang until five o'clock in the morning, sharing the message of Jesus Christ.

One of the things which most impressed me was the reception we received from these people. After our performance, the husband of Mockfudava, the foremost contemporary composer in the USSR, came to our European director and told him, "You know, I am a poet.

Words are my stock in trade. One word that is overused in English is the word beautiful.'' But then he went on to say, ''I do not believe in God. I've been taught all my life that there is no God. But when I watched those young people stand on that platform, raise their hands, and worship an entity that I do not even believe exists, there is only one word that I can use to describe what I saw. It is the word beautiful.''

In 1981 I was sitting in my home in Tulsa, Oklahoma, when our team phoned from Helsinki, Finland. They said, ''Terry, we're on our way back into Moscow. We have no bookings; we're just going in as the Spirit directs.''

I had just been reading out of 2 Chronicles, chapter 20, so I read it to them over the phone: *And when he* (Jehoshaphat) *had consulted with the people, he appointed singers unto the Lord, and that should praise the beauty of holiness, as they went out before the army, and to say, Praise the Lord; for his mercy endureth for ever* (v. 21).

''The singers marched before the army of the Lord,'' I said. ''I want you guys singing in the Spirit all the way to Moscow, and let's trust God that when you get there He's going to do the unusual.''

When the team arrived in Moscow they called up a few friends. One of the young men they phoned was one of the youth editors of *Pravda*, the largest newspaper in the world, with a circulation of 16 million. The young man's name was Yuri, and he had been impressed by our group during our visit a year before. The team said, ''Yuri, we have no place to rehearse, we'd like a place to practice.''

He said, ''I'll see what I can find out.''

About two hours later Yuri called back and said, ''You're not going to believe it, but the central television studio downtown is open. Nobody is in there today and they said it would be alright if you came in and practiced your music there.''

So the team went in and began to rehearse. When the producers heard them, they came out from everywhere to listen. They said, ''What is this? We've never heard music like this before in our lives. Would you mind if we filmed it?''

· The next evening our team walked into a live studio, in the heart of Moscow, to be filmed while singing the Gospel message of Jesus Christ. That is truly amazing, considering that the central television studio is the only television chain in the entire USSR! They don't have three networks as we do — only one. And our team was performing on it!

Besides that, as the team walked into the studio, they found that 500 people had gathered to hear them. These were the elite of Russian society — the aristocrats, the intelligensia, the artists and poets of the nation. They were all seated in the audience as Living Sound came on to perform.

One of our young ladies told me afterwards, ''Terry, we didn't know what was going to happen. We prayed quietly backstage and just said, 'God, it's up to You, it's in Your hands.' ''

They walked out and began to sing. They had developed a repertoire of nine charismatic worship choruses in the Russian language. The audience clapped as they began to sing their upbeat music. Then when they came to a certain place in their presentation, all of a sudden they changed gears. They began to sing in the Russian language, and they began to praise the Lord. They raised their hands and began to worship God. There were four or five television cameras recording the concert, filming everything that was going on. That television program was aired in Russia on January 2, 1982. It covered the entire Soviet bloc. There on Russian television were American Christian young people, with hands raised in the air, worshipping and praising God! And it was seen by millions all across Russia! This Gospel is going through all the earth! God is moving by His Spirit!

2
The Weapons of Our Warfare

Now, let me explain why I have shared with you these stories from my own past experience. Back in the days when these things were happening, I didn't really know what I was doing or what the team was doing. I didn't realize the power of praise to tear down strongholds — spiritual strongholds — established by the devil. I knew that we were to praise God, that we were to pray in our prayer language, that we were to honor the Holy Ghost. I had known all those things since the time I was a little child. But I did not fully understand the principle of spiritual warfare involved, the weapons placed at the disposal of the believer.

Now, because of what the Lord has revealed to me through such experiences, I have come to understand these things. Because of that knowledge and understanding, my team and I are much better equipped now for victorious Christian living and ministry. In the months ahead our team will be going back to Poland and to Russia and to other nations behind the Iron Curtain. In a sense, we will be marching into the middle of the lion's den. But this time we have some weapons to unleash, weapons that I understand better. So we go now in the power and confidence of the Holy Spirit.

In these pages I would like to share with you

what the Lord has revealed to me from His Word concerning spiritual warfare.

Our Three Weapons

Let's look again at our scripture text, 2 Corinthians 10:4: *(For the weapons of our warfare are not carnal, but mighty through God to the pulling down of strong holds.)* Notice that we Christians are equipped with weapons, mighty weapons which are able to tear down strongholds set up by the enemy, Satan.

What are our weapons? How do we identify them? I think there is a great misunderstanding in the Body of Christ as to what our spiritual weapons really are. Many people say that prayer is a spiritual weapon — it is not. Some people would say that speaking in tongues is a spiritual weapon — it is not.

There are three things identified in the Word of God as spiritual weapons for use by believers: 1) the Word of God, 2) the Name of Jesus, and 3) the Blood of Christ. Let's look at each one of these very briefly.

The Word of God is a weapon. It's a sword. Paul writes in Ephesians 6:17: *And take the helmet of salvation, and the sword of the Spirit, which is the word of God.* Hebrews 4:12 tells us: *The word of God is quick, and powerful, and sharper than any twoedged sword, piercing even to the dividing asunder of soul and spirit, and of the joints and marrow . . .*

Our second weapon is the Name of Jesus. As believers we have the right to use that Name to defeat Satan and to destroy his works and power. In Mark 16:17-18 Jesus commissioned us and granted us power of attorney to use His name against the enemy:

And these signs shall follow them that believe; In my name shall they cast out devils; they shall speak with new tongues;

They shall take up serpents; and if they drink any deadly thing it shall not hurt them; they shall lay hands on the sick, and they shall recover.

Thirdly, the Blood of Christ is a spiritual weapon. In Revelation 12:11 we read that *they* (the saints of God) *overcame him* (Satan) *by the blood of the Lamb, and by the word of their testimony.*

These three weapons of the Word, the Name and the Blood are for the believer to use to overcome our enemy and to tear down his strongholds in our own lives and in the lives of others. As we learn how to use the weapons, we move into a power with God that we've never known before.

Weapons Activators

Now we have four activators or "launching pads" for these weapons, things which activate our weapons against the devil. The first is prayer; the second is testimony or witness; the third is preaching; and the fourth is praise.

In the past there has been a great deal of

preaching and teaching about the Word of God, and that is good. God's Word is a weapon and we should know about it and use it. I am sure that from your own experience you have seen your confession of the Word bring you out of sickness and disease and bondage to the devil. No doubt, you have been using this weapon to good advantage by believing and confessing it with your mouth. You have undoubtedly found out that it is a powerful force against the wiles of the enemy. You have probably availed yourself of it many times to destroy the strongholds and power of the evil one.

But the Word of God is just one part of the paraphernalia that God has given to the Church. He has other elements that He wants to bring into the total equation so we can catch a glimpse of all that He has in mind for the Body of Christ. I believe God has some new things that He is introducing to us today. One of these is the launching pad of prayer.

Great men of God, pastors and teachers everywhere are saying that God is bringing prayer — intercessory prayer — prayer like we've never known before — back to the body of Christ. That is true. If we want to see God move, we are going to have to get involved more in prayer, the kind of prayer that shakes strongholds. We can do it individually in our own prayer closets, or corporately in churches or other such group meetings.

Prayer changes things, that is true. But in

order to change things, prayer has got to hurl weapons. It's no good to pray traditionally. Staid, lifeless, mundane, effortless prayers will never defeat the enemy nor shake him loose from his hold on this world. It's going to take more than that to make him let go of his prey. In your praying, if you are not actively throwing the Word, the Name or the Blood at the devil or his strongholds, then your prayer will have no effect.

To accomplish anything, prayer has got to use a weapon. That's what gives it power.

The same is true of your testimony. When you testify concerning the Word, the power of God goes forth. When you testify concerning the Name, the power of God goes forth. That's why Jesus said, "These signs shall follow them that believe; In *My Name* . . ." That's the weapon! The Name of Jesus. That is what Jesus meant. He was telling us to throw the weapon first, and then the devil has to bow.

It is not enough just to pray, or to testify or give witness. We must have something on which to base our prayer, on which to base our testimony. Otherwise our prayer and testimony have no power behind them.

The third launching pad for our spiritual weapons is preaching. This refers to those who have a special call of God upon their lives to announce or proclaim the Word of God, the Good News of the Gospel of Jesus Christ. But again, it is not the preaching of the Gospel that has the power — it is the Gospel itself which is the power. Paul said: *For I am not ashamed of the gospel of Christ: for it is the power of God unto salvation . . .* (Rom. 1:16). But in order for that Gospel power to be effective, it must be put into action through preaching. As a force, it must be launched into action.

Praise

Now let's look at the fourth launching pad — praise. Have you noticed that all four launching pads for God's weapons have to do with the mouth? Prayer, testimony or witnessing or confession, preaching, praise — every one of these have to do with the mouth. Your mouth is tied up with your spiritual victory or your spiritual defeat.

Praise is a launching pad for spiritual weapons. I believe that God is bringing this truth to the Body of Christ in our generation. I believe that God is going to help us as Christians to learn to focus our praise in such an acute and powerful way that we can use it like a laser to totally devastate the strongholds and power of Satan. We can learn to focus our faith against disease, against depression, against poverty, against bondage, against whatever the stronghold is, and annihilate it completely. As we Christians learn to take authority over strongholds of the enemy we will see the glory of God demonstrated in our lives as never before, as the power and glory of God moves through us in our praise.

Praise is one way God wants to bring victory to His Church. Just one way. One delivery system. Each one is important. Each one must be emphasized. But it is vitally important to recognize and remember that praise is in the Word of God from cover to cover. If we don't understand the place and importance of praise to God, if we don't get ahold of that truth, we will never understand what God is trying to say to His Body in these last days.

Here are some facts about praise. I'm sure that you have probably heard them all of your life. First of all, the Bible says that God inhabits the praises of His people. Now what does that mean? The *New International Version* says that God sits enthroned upon praise. When we praise God as a body, God Himself comes into our midst. We set up a throne in our midst, and God Himself comes down to occupy that place of honor and authority. Now we have all heard a great deal lately about the "glory cloud of God" coming down. We are going to see that glory cloud when God comes down to inhabit the praises of His people. We are going to see it right before our very eyes. Because God does inhabit the praises of His people.

There is really no use in our praying for the sick, believing God for deliverance, believing God for the miraculous, until we've turned our spirits loose in praise that brings us before the throne, because it is that praise that brings God into our midst.

That's the first fact of praise, that God inhabits it. The second fact of praise is simple. There is a certain protocol to be followed in order to come before the King of Kings.

In 1980 our team was invited to come to Rome as the guests of Pope John Paul II to sing at St. Peter's Square. The Pope had heard about us back in 1972 while we were singing in that Polish nightclub, when we had blown things up by praise, not really knowing that we were taking authority over strongholds. The Pope, who at that time was just Karol Cardinal Wojtyla, the head of the Roman Catholic Church in southern Poland, heard about this group of crazy Americans called Living Sound, and he wanted to meet us. In 1975 we met him in Czestochowa. Then in 1976 we met him again. He invited us into his home and gave us fellowship, played the guitar, learned some charismatic choruses. It turned out that he had bought all of our albums, because he liked our music. He has since given us his apostolic blessing to take the Gospel through the Roman Catholic Church around the world, for which honor and opportunity we give glory to God.

But do you know what moved the heart of this great religious leader? The thing that moved his heart was praise. He was impressed and touched by the worship and praise he saw in us and in our singing.

When I came to meet the Pope in Rome in

1980, I was taken aside by his personal secretary, Monsignor Monducci. I was instructed in the various items of protocol that are necessary to follow in meeting a dignitary such as the Pope. If you are invited to meet the President of the United States, for example, you would be instructed by one of his aides in the proper way to approach the President.

That is exactly what the Word of God gives us. It outlines for us the proper manner to be followed in coming before the Father God. It provides us with a lesson in protocol. And do you know what the protocol is? *Enter into his gates with thanksgiving, and into his courts with praise* (Ps. 100:4)!

There is only one way to come before the King, and that is with praise. And that is not just good manners or proper etiquette. That is the law of God, the principle of God.

The Sacrifice of Praise

Although praise is demanded of us by God, it does not go unrewarded. In Isaiah 61:3 the prophet, speaking for the Lord, tells us that a Redeemer has been sent to us so that we may exchange *the garment of praise for the spirit of heaviness.* A garment is something we wear, something we put on.

There is a spirit of heaviness loose in America today. There is a spirit of financial depression, a spirit of economic unrest, a spirit of fear about the future. People are afraid of the conflict in Central America, afraid of the Soviet Union, afraid of what's happening around the world. There is a real spirit of anxiety at work in our land. You can easily catch that spirit just by watching the evening news.

But the Bible tells us Christians to put off the spirit of heaviness and to put on the garment of praise. When you got dressed today, what did you do? You walked into your closet and picked out a dress or a suit or whatever you have on right now. You chose what kind of clothes you were going to wear for that day. It was a conscious choice, based not upon your feelings but upon your will or volition. So it is with praise. We don't praise God because we necessarily feel like praising God, or because praise is something that suits our emotional frame of mind at that particular moment. There are times when praise doesn't even occur to us. It may not be something that we want to do right then. But the Word says that we are to put on the garment of praise. So we do it. We put on praise just like we put on a coat or a dress. We clothe ourselves in praise. By a conscious act of the will.

As we put on the garment of praise and learn to focus that praise against Satan's strongholds, we will begin to walk in victory and power. Those strongholds are going to be blown apart by the power of praise coming from the lips and the hearts of God's children!

Now I realize that sometimes it is hard to

praise. But Hebrews 13:15 says: *Let us offer the sacrifice of praise to God continually, that is, the fruit of our lips, giving* (confessing) *thanks to his name.*

That word "sacrifice" is tied in with praise throughout the entire Bible. There are times when it pains us to praise. There are times when we hurt and we don't want to praise God because the hurt is so intense. That is when praise to God is a sacrifice, because making a sacrifice means doing something you don't want to do or don't feel like doing, giving up the fulfillment of your own desires for the benefit of someone else.

"Let us offer the sacrifice of praise to God *continually.*" This means that we are to be praising God all the time — every day — moment by moment. We are to walk in praise, live in praise, cloak ourselves with praise, confessing thanks to His Name.

I was impressed by something I heard Oral Roberts say concerning Jonah in the belly of the whale. In the final verse before he was vomitted up on dry land, the Bible says that Jonah promised God, *I will pay that that I have vowed* (Jonah 2:9). In other words, Jonah was saying, "Okay, God, You win! I will do what You say. I will be obedient as I have promised."

But that verse also says something else. Just before Jonah said, "I will pay that that I have vowed," he said, *I will sacrifice unto thee with the voice of thanksgiving.* And when he said that, he hit the "hot button," and the whale vomitted

31

him up on dry land. Why? Because that fish could not handle somebody who was praising God!

Now, there's really no good reason to praise God when you've been in the belly of a fish with seaweed wrapped around your neck for three days. Jonah was stubborn. He didn't flow in praise at all. It took him three days of misery to begin to pray. I believe that if I had been in his shoes I would have been praying 50 seconds on the way down that fish's throat! But not Jonah. It took him three days before he got it through his head what he needed to do. So then, finally, he prayed and told God, ''Lord, I'll pay my vow. I will offer unto You the sacrifice of thanksgiving.'' When he did that, the whale got rid of him like a hot potato. He couldn't handle him any more.

That's what happens to the power of the enemy who has you bound. When you exercise the weapon at your disposal, you get out of his hold and you tear down his strongholds upon you!

In Acts, chapter 16, we read where Paul and Silas were thrown in prison in Philippi after casting a demon out of a young girl. They were taken prisoner by the Roman authority, tied up, lashed across their backs with the Roman cat-o'-nine-tails, and placed in a prison cell in stocks.

Now by all rights, these men could have been complaining to God about the missionary business. "Lord, I don't want to be a missionary. It's too hard, it hurts too much." That's what they could have been doing, but it's not what they were doing. What were they doing in those trying circumstances? The Bible says in Acts 16:25: *And at midnight Paul and Silas prayed, and sang praises unto God . . .*

What do you praise God for when your back is lashed? What do you praise God for when you're hurting all over, when your feet are locked in stocks, when you're in prison with a bunch of criminals? What do you praise God for when it seems that everything is going against you? Frankly I don't know. I don't know *what* Paul and Silas praised God *for,* but I know *why* they praised Him — because God said to praise Him!

And they didn't just sing a little chorus softly to themselves either. They threw back their shoulders and sang boldly because the Bible records: *. . . and the prisoners heard them.*

Was it worth it to Paul and Silas to praise God? Did it do any good? Did it really accomplish anything other than making them feel better about their situation? Let's look at verse 26 and see:

And suddenly there was a great earthquake, so that the foundations of the prison were shaken; and immediately all the doors were opened, and every one's bonds were loosed.

When Paul and Silas began to pray and praise God with all their hearts, God looked down from out of heaven, saw two missionaries with their backs lashed to shreds, and said, ''If those two can sing praises to me in that kind of situation, then I'm going to join them!'' And God started to sing along with Paul and Silas. And when God sings, He sings bass! The ground began to tremble, and the prison walls began to shake, and all the doors and bonds were burst open!

Now that's not in the text, of course, but I like to think that perhaps that's what really happened. Because it illustrates my point. When Paul and Silas began to praise God in the midst of their trial, God heard them and He honored their sacrifice of praise.

God will always honor the sacrifice of praise by His children. As Christians we need to learn what our spiritual weapons are and how to activate them to tear down the strongholds of Satan in our lives which keep us bound.

3
The Power of Praise

Some time ago I was in London, England, to attend a board meeting. I had been in that meeting all day and had just come back to my hotel room and gone to bed. I had been asleep about thirty minutes when one of the men from our office walked into my room and shook me awake.

"Terry," he said, "I have some terrible news for you. We've just received word that your wife, Jan, had an automobile wreck. She was thrown through the windshield and has gone on to be with the Lord."

Later I was told that I sat there in bed for ten minutes in a state of total shock. I remember thinking over and over, "No, it's not true. I'm going to go back to sleep and wake up and this whole thing will go away." But it was true, and it didn't go away. I finally had to pull myself together and call my three children and tell them what had happened. I've never done anything so hard in all my life.

On the plane coming back home I said, "God, it's not fair. I have done everything I know to do. I have been obedient and taken Your Word. I've gone to the ends of the earth to proclaim Your Gospel. Five times I have been interrogated by the Russian KGB. I've gone into areas where no other man has ever preached the Gospel message. But now, I'm done, I'm through!''

Oral Roberts spoke at the memorial service for my wife. Then several days later, I was still in such inner turmoil that I went to talk with Brother Roberts because I knew that he had lost his eldest son just a few months before. We sat in his office, tears in our eyes, and talked.

Brother Roberts said, ''Terry, I want to tell you something.'' And he stood up. We were in his private office on the seventh floor overlooking the magnificent campus of ORU and the City of Faith. Brother Roberts looked out the window, and then he turned to me, motioned with his hand, and said, ''Do you see all this?'' And he began to name different aspects of his tremendous ministry and different buildings on the sprawling campus. ''Every one of these projects, everything that I have ever done, has come out of some sort of turmoil in my life. They came out of my spirit, when I began to pray in other tongues and to interpret back what I had prayed in the Spirit.''

He paused for a moment to reflect. Then he looked at me and said, ''Terry, if you will do this one thing, it will save your life — learn how to pray in the Spirit and how to interpret back what God is saying to you.''

For the next three months I was on an emotional roller coaster, but I never forgot what this great man of God had told me. The next morning I got up at six o'clock in the morning and I prayed for two hours.

Now I didn't want to pray. I was mad. I was angry and hurt. My heart was aching within me so badly I didn't think I could stand it. I really didn't have any desire to talk to God. All I could think about was my terrible burden and pain. But I made up my mind, "I'm going to pray in the Spirit." And I did. I prayed, and I prayed, and I prayed. I prayed until I sensed within my spirit that I had come to the point where the Father wanted to speak back to me.

When I got to that place, I opened my Bible and pointed to 1 Corinthians 14:13: *Wherefore let him that speaketh in an unknown tongue pray that he may interpret.* I said, "Father, it's in Your Word, and I'm going to do it. By faith, I am now going to interpret my own prayer."

As I began to interpret in English, the words began to flow out of my spirit, out of my heart, and there was the healing power of God for my need. God began to minister to me through the words of the Holy Spirit, the Comforter. Then the Lord said to me, "Son, I'm going to lead you into a ministry of healing; I'm going to lead you into a ministry of casting out devils; and I'm going to do it through worship and praise."

I answered, "But Lord, I don't feel like worshipping and praising."

"That's alright," He told me, "I'm going to show you how."

After that experience, the Lord led me through a special personal Holy Ghost schooling on worship and praise.

The Wave of God

Some months later there was a special meeting for charismatic leaders from across the nation. Many directors of international ministries, as well as many leading pastors from throughout the country were in attendance. The primary topic of our discussion was, what is God saying to His Church today. I asked these great men of faith this question: "What is the prophetic word coming from God to you men who are leaders across our nation?"

Without exception, they all gave the same answer: "We believe that we are on the crest of a wave of worship and praise that is so over-whelming and so powerful that it will become the power and the source of evangelism in the Church."

One pastor summarized it for us this way: "When people in the world see people in the Church so in love with their Father that worship and praise become the hallmark, the identifying characteristic, of their lives, then the world is going to beat down the walls of the church to get in because they are going to want what the Church has!"

All of these men agreed that in the days ahead praise is going to become the power and the flow and the force of evangelism. The new wave of God in the Body of Christ in the 1980's will spring forth out of worship and praise. That

wave is coming. It's on the way. In fact, it has
already begun.

God Honors His Word

Since that meeting I have started doing
something I had never done before. I have
taken all of our songs by Living Sound and
arranged them so that every one of them is a
song of praise and worship to God. I preach a
simple salvation message and invite people to
come to Christ. As a result, I have seen
hundreds respond and be saved and healed.

We have ordered our services so that
everything we do is structured to lead people
into the presence of God. We have decided that
we are going to tear down spiritual strongholds
in every service through worship and praise.
We are seeing the saving and healing power of
God manifested in every service. Because God
has promised it.

*For it shall come to pass in that day, saith the
Lord of hosts, that I will break his yoke from off thy
neck, and will burst thy bonds . . . .*

*For I am with thee, saith the Lord, to save thee
. . . .*

*For I will restore health unto thee, and I will heal
thee of thy wounds, saith the Lord . . . .*

*And out of them shall proceed thanksgiving and
the voice of them that make merry: and I will
multiply them, and they shall not be few; I will also
glorify them, and they shall not be small.*

Jeremiah 30:8,11,17,19

God has promised that if we will praise and worship Him that He will break Satan's yoke from us, restore health to us, bless us with thanksgiving and joy, and increase our numbers. And God has got to honor His Word.

Now I am a Canadian. I come from Western Canada and I know that a prophet is not without honor except in his own country. I decided that if I could accomplish this at home, I could do it anywhere. So recently we took our team up to Canada for six weeks. We toured some of the major churches in my home area. What I saw happen totally astounded me.

While in a church in Edmonton, Alberta, a healing service was held. The elders anointed people with oil, and as far as I could see, nothing happened. But later as Living Sound began to sing we turned that audience loose in praise and worship. People began to lay hands on each other for healing. The results were tremendous.

All of a sudden, over on one side of the auditorium a lady began to scream, "I can see! I can see!" We didn't know what all the commotion was about. The ushers were trying to quiet her down, but she was too excited to be hushed up. And for good reason. For the first time in her life, she could see, and she was hysterical with joy!

A man started to jump up and down and wave his arm around wildly. He came running down to the altar to give his testimony. He said that while working on a construction job some time earlier a pipe had fallen 110 feet and had broken his shoulder and arm. He had been on workmen's compensation for seven months and in constant pain. That arm and shoulder were totally healed by the power of God in a moment, in the act of praise and worship.

All over that audience, people were pulling hearing aids out of their ears, healed by the power of God. One lady in the service, the church secretary, was so sick she didn't even feel like praying for herself. She was scheduled to go to the hospital for major surgery the next morning. She was reaching out to pray for someone else in the congregation when she felt the healing power of the Lord go through her own body. The next day she went in for what was to have been a 20-minute operation. But when the doctors opened her up, they spent an hour trying to find her problem, but could not locate one thing wrong with her. She had been totally healed by the power of God. And all she had done was to pray for someone else's healing.

That whole meeting was so exciting we could hardly stand it. It is thrilling to see God move upon His people in such a miraculous way in response to praise and worship. We proved there and elsewhere that God does indeed honor His Word, if His people will only take Him at His Word and praise Him.

Taking Authority Through Praise

In Campmeeting in Tulsa, Oklahoma, in 1983, Dr. Kenneth Hagin prophesied over me. He prophesied that this message that God has laid on my heart, this message which we are taking to the Body of Christ and which I am sharing with you in these pages, will go forth into every area of the world. I praise God for that confirmation of His call upon my life. I firmly intend to fulfill that calling.

In the future we are going to wrap all our crusades, both at home and abroad, around praise and worship. In the Soviet Union, throughout Europe and Africa, and everywhere God sends us, we're simply going to bring people into the presence of God and let Him take it from there. We are going to take authority over the strongholds of Satan in the lives of people because we know that they cannot stand any longer when God's people are flowing in praise.

I remember one time when we were ministering in a church in Eugene, Oregon. On Sunday morning, the pastor of that church stood up and said, ''Folks, pray for me. One of the church elders has been getting a sense in the spirit that there is going to be an assassination attempt on my life. I don't know what to do about it. But I've prayed and I want you to pray with me.''

In that series of meetings, we were holding deliverance services every night in which we cast out evil spirits and prayed for the sick. On a Tuesday night, I was dealing with people who were oppressed of the devil. As I came walking out of the deliverance room late that evening, a lady came up to me and said, ''Brother Terry, you've got to pray with me.''

I said, ''I'm sorry, Ma'am, I can't pray for anybody right now. I've got to get home, I'm dead tired.''

''But you've just got to talk to me,'' she insisted. So we sat down together and she began to relate her story to me. She said, ''I can't remember a thing that happened in my life from the time I was a child until I was 18 years of age. My whole childhood is a blank. I have asked my mother what happened many times, but she always tells me, 'I don't want you to know . . . it's too terrible.' ''

I asked her, ''Do you feel that you're oppressed by the devil?''

''Yes,'' she replied. ''I'm a member of this church, but I am oppressed by Satan.''

''Alright then,'' I told her, ''let's do something about it right now.'' And I began to take authority over the spirits that were tormenting her. The first spirit which manifested itself was hatred. It came out of her at my command. But I knew in my spirit that there was something still there, something even more evil than a spirit of hatred.

''Spirit,'' I commanded, ''Whatever your name is, I want to know that name now!''

Suddenly a deep, bass voice said to me, "I am going to murder the pastor! I am going to murder the pastor!"

At once I boldly declared, "You lying demon, you're not going to murder anybody! You're coming out of her right now, in the Name of Jesus!"

That thing shook the lady like a little rag doll, and came out of her. She began to cry and weep and shake all over. I asked her what was wrong and she told me, "Every night for the past three weeks that spirit has come to me and told me that I've got to kill the pastor. I finally gave in. I was making plans to kill him this week."

"You're not going to do it now, are you?" I asked.

"No," she said, "I am not."

The next night she was back in the service, with both hands raised in the air, praising the Lord. Later she went for counseling to the very pastor she had been going to kill.

But the thing that gave me the boldness to take authority over those lying demons of hatred and murder came as a direct result of praise and worship to God.

If you want to tear down the strongholds in your life or in the lives of others, then praise and worship is the answer you are seeking. Get to know your spiritual weapons and how to activate and use them against the enemy. Take the weapons of the Word of God, the Name of

Jesus, and the Blood of Christ, and direct them at the enemy from the launching pad of praise.

Learn to direct your praise — to focus it — for maximum effect. When you praise God you are training your spiritual weapons on the strongholds of Satan and tearing them down.

Praise the Lord!

Pope John Paul II invited LIVING SOUND to perform a special concert in St. Peter's Square in August of 1980. Even though the singing group is Protestant, he has personally recommended Living Sound's apostolic ministry to the Church at large.

About the Author

Terry Law, president and founder of Terry Law Ministries, has become one of America's foremost speakers on Praise and Worship.

In the late 1960's, Terry Law began an international missionary team called Living Sound. With a special emphasis in world missions, he has led Living Sound teams to minister in over forty countries of the world, seeing multiplied thousands of people accept Jesus Christ as Savior. His work continues through Living Sound Europe, Living Sound Russia, and Living Sound Poland.

Terry and his wife, Shirley, and their six children reside in Tulsa, Oklahoma. Through his world headquarters in Tulsa, he coordinates the multi-faceted outreaches of the ministry and ministers worldwide in the areas of Praise and Worship and missions with a special emphasis on healing.

For a complete list of tapes and books by Terry Law, including the following new releases:

Praise Releases Faith
by Terry Law

and

Yet Will I Praise Him
by Terry and Shirley Law

write to:
LAW OUTREACH MINISTRIES
P.O. Box 3563
Tulsa, Oklahoma 74101